The Seven Day Marriage

A Life Journey Travel Guide

By Jeremiah Hutchins

and Nick Delmedico

Published by

Copyright ©2023

Contact: halfabook@dplus2.com

All rights reserved under International and Pan-American Copyright Conventions. No part of this publication may be produced, stored in a retrieval system, or transmitted in any form or by any means, electronic, mechanical, photocopying, recording, scanning, or otherwise, except as permitted under sections 107 and 108 of the 1976 United States Copyright Act, without the prior written permission of the publisher.

Manufactured in the United States of America

The Seven Day Marriage

ISBN 978-1-58884-029-5

Self Improvement

Psychology

CONTENTS

Introduction

DISCLAIMER: I believe that most relationship books focus too much on what's wrong with us or how we are supposed to look on our journey through life. Even though we strive to understand the different personalities and character traits that we all possess, we can still manage to find a partner who is not true to themselves and does not respect themselves as an important individual. I am not writing this book to avoid going to a counselor or psychologist, but to maybe limit whether we need to go. Just because we have the wrong person with us on our daily journey does not mean we have to abort the trip.

Through my extensive research I discovered couples that have such opposite career paths and outside interests that it makes me wonder how they can enjoy some of the same activities, let alone a lifestyle when they are together. This appears to be the key: to successfully be together, a couple must embrace their differences and their similarities at the same time. Communication and acceptance must be present for a healthy relationship to thrive.

This book offers insight into my research. I will cite examples and case studies from couples I have come to know and forget. The results can help the reader learn how to have a healthy and happy relationship, friendship, marriage, business arrangement, or whatever you choose to call it. By following my Seven Day Marriage plan, you can test your resolve and better determine if you have a future together. Or maybe dodge a costly mistake.

Jeremiah Hutchins
April 2023

PART I

Chapter 1
Why I Dislike Self Help Books

The important thing is not to stop questioning. Curiosity has its own reason for existing. One cannot help but be in awe when he contemplates the mysteries of eternity, of life, of the marvelous structure of reality. It is enough if one tries merely to comprehend a little of this mystery every day.
— Albert Einstein, Life magazine, May 2, 1955

I have read more than my share of self-help books, and they all seem to have a common theme. The basic assumption of a self-help book is that there is something wrong with you that needs fixing. True, we're not all perfect beings, and who among us is without flaws, but this is no reason to tear down your self-image and rework it into something more palatable for someone else or for society. There is an old saying: “To thine own self be true.”

That said, this book is intended to be a *self improvement book*, and not a *self help book*. Self help sounds too much like a plea. Self improvement is something we all embrace and something most of us want to do. I believe that marriage, more than anything else, can trigger the need for self improvement.

Many times I have seen that the changes needed to sustain a healthy marriage, when they do occur, often follow the divorce. I believe that is because of pride and the human reaction to asking for help. If this resonates with you, then embark on the path of self improvement. Sometimes, cleaning up your own garbage can inspire your partner to do the same.

We are indelibly locked into a human form that functions well in this world of physical wants and needs. Behind each face is a being that lives alone in this shell. We interact, but do we really know and understand what each of us experiences in this world of isolation? The amount of this world we share with others is completely up to us. Despite empathy and imagination, none of us really knows what the other is going through on the inside. As intimate as we get, there is still a great distance between us.

Knowing that, why do we judge ourselves so harshly? Unless you are a psychopath with anti-social behaviors, you engage in an inner dialog that shapes your beliefs. If society tells you that you are overweight, do you accept that judgment? What if another person tells you that? What if your partner tells you that it doesn't matter? Do you still believe them? In the end, ask yourself, who sets these standards?

True, we all are prey to the lemming mentality. We have a desire to be “normal”, but what is that? As it is impossible to include everyone, statisticians take sample populations to analyze. This creates an arbitrary “normal” that becomes a reference point to mark out standard deviations. You may feel like a standard deviant, but the fact is you may not even be a part of the sample population chosen for the study. The point is, everyone belongs somewhere. Finding that special person or place is up to you. Nobody can truly define “normal.”

Something I don't like about self-help books is the fluff that is built around a single, simple idea. I found myself reading through a hundred pages to get to the few sentences that have meaning for me. Why not cut to the chase? Well, that's what I've done in this book. Instead of one single idea, I've peppered this text with hundreds of ideas. Feel free to pick and choose. Write things on slips of paper and post them prominently. Share these ideas with others.

So, why bother reading this book?

Maybe you're addicted to self-help books, eternally caught in the mindset that there is something wrong with you that needs fixing. What if that was a lie, a self delusion that you somehow got trapped into thinking? Maybe it was some rules of society you thought you were following, or maybe a controlling relationship, be it partner or parent. Somewhere along your path you learned to believe you are broken.

This may be a reason to seek professional help. Beware though: addiction is powerful, whether it be a craving for love, drugs, excitement, food, tattoos, or even an addiction to therapy. In the long run, this book may be cheaper than a single counseling session. Like therapy, this book requires honesty and commitment. Why not start with learning something about yourself?

And there's another problem. We may learn things about ourselves. People may point out our faults, but how often do we act on them? Even more importantly: how often do we recognize them? Denial is a powerful thing. In order to have a successful relationship with anyone, we need to be clear about who we are and what we represent.

With this book, all we ask is you be yourself. Your honest self. We often hide things from our partners and loved ones. The reasons can be complicated: fear of discovery, protecting someone from the "truth", personal gain or loss at stake, avoiding family drama, we even go against the grain of our personality for whatever crazy reason. Just be honest.

The Seven Day Marriage requires honesty. If you can't be honest with another person for seven days, how can you expect it to last a lifetime? This is rule number one and it acts in reverse. Be honest with yourself!

There are other reasons to follow the guidance in this book. Marriages are expensive. How many parents have paid for an expensive wedding, sacrificing their own comfort for their children's happiness, only to find it was over in six months to a year? If only they had bought this book instead, at most they would be out the cost of an expensive vacation.

Undoing a mistake can be difficult. The cost of divorce, both in money and emotional capital, can far exceed the price of a wedding. Again, I offer you the Seven Day Marriage as a way of testing your resolve without going broke.

Either way, you'll come out ahead, both financially and emotionally.

But only if you're honest!

Chapter 2
The Many Types of Relationships

A heart is not judged by how much you love, but by how much you are loved by others.

The Wizard of Oz to the Tin Man

There are as many types of relationships as there are people. As society and people change, so do relationships. In this respect there is no “normal”. Reflect for a moment what it must have been like for your parents or grandparents. Were they not bound by the rules of the society in which they lived? We've all heard about shotgun weddings, but what about other cultures? Could you live in an arranged marriage with a partner chosen for you?

Many things in most civilized democratic societies

contribute to our image of a relationship So, let's get into some of the culprits who rub up against that. The damage they do can be a lesson to those that seek a healthy and loveing partner. Some people learn by reading, some by lecture, and others by hard knocks experience. Over and over, I'm afraid, till we get it right. Here are a few I have run across in my search for true friendship.

If you encounter these types: Read the warning label first.

Alcoholic/Addict--- RUN AND DON'T LOOK BACK UNLESS YOU ARE ONE... The end of this chapter. No seriously, you can buy a new car every year on the cost alone. Why and how we get here is for me boredom. I love to go out and people watch. Scary sometimes, but for the most part funny and entertaining. It's interesting how we categorize all our different traits and then package them like securities; but, they are actually our insecurities, and we cherish them. The thought of being with someone that does not function well without alcohol is disturbing to say the least. How did we get to this point that we can justify such behavior in a moment's thought and then believe that it is better?

Baggage Cart You can almost feel the weight. Make no doubt about it, you will be carrying it too, one piece at a time until you acquire all the traits of a bellboy turned pack animal. If you have your own baggage, leave it at the doorway. Marriage starts best with a clean slate. The past cannot be changed. Forgive yourself and your partner and move on to a better life.

Don't Buy Friends: It's cheaper to make new ones. Don't be the person who runs from every situation when they realize, in a moment of clear insight, that it's not them, but the mirror of the other person. You will be a slave on either side of this one's audience. You will be worrying about the other person's happiness, feelings, needs, and so on, and soon forget your worry is *the* worry. Confused? Change or run please.

Entrapment: Did you wake up with a diamond studded dog collar around your neck this morning? Finding yourself on a short leash? Obedience training usually follows as you learn where and when you can perform your tricks. This may not be for you, but there are some who love the comfort of a close cage. Other forms of entrapment include pregnancy, bribes, promises, and coercion.

Haters: To see one of these may be rare, unless your law of attraction is going off like a beacon, you will most likely hear about one. This is the person that can flip on a dime and all hell breaks loose. I would rather get the hanger from mommy dearest than go through another demeaning scream fest. No thank you. We have this local girl that when she gets lit, likes to spit on you and then get snotty with all possible bystanders. I like the stories of the amazing claw marks left behind. Be honest, is it worth it?

Judgers: This can be anyone, even one who goes to the church down the street - my favorite to pick out of the crowd. Relationships in a small town kill you in one bad night of decision. Maybe you get two bad decisions, but once word gets around, it's hard to change the image projected onto you. It's a disease taught and mastered by the best. Judgers can look at every person who comes in range of them, and something will be wrong with everyone: gums, nose, magic mirror disease, shoes, past dates. Just remember faking the smile and small talk is another craft mastered by the best. If you do encounter one of these, remember the old adage: Judge not lest ye be judged. Good advice, as judging and comparing yourself to others just leads to confusion and a muddy self image.

The Meme Generator or "SHARE" person: Holy cow. How many friends do we have, and be honest, the single ones can also make up or share the most ritual love, hate, confused, backstabbing memes for all to see. Even the video to end the relationship forever. Thank God for artificial dating otherwise we'd have more Lorena Bobbitts out there. If you are too young or too old to remember Lorena, she's still lurking on the internet.

Low Self-esteem generally runs on the heavy side of why we may be constantly searching for the happiness pill. I still can't believe that Barbie or Ken has stepped into this shadow too, without even knowing why. Both sexes on this topic should be taken with caution. A partner that continually suffers from this disease can be hard to cure. A relationship, with all its expectations and pressures, may not be what is needed. A best friend can be just the right medicine, or in this case, perhaps even a good therapist.

Mama's Boy: Do your own damn laundry, learn to cook and scratch front and back. These ones are messy, but if you are on the other side of this missing puzzle, this can be very therapeutic and you could end up helping each other. If not, welcome to the maid brigade. Your best friend and new companion will be Mr. Clean in the large, economy sized bottle.

Needy is the beggar down the street. "You can't sell that around here!" I scream out the window while driving by. Have the meal ready when you get off work, while sitting at your front door uninvited. Wow, that could be the special person to spend the rest of your life, maybe as a doormat.

Pathological Liar: storyteller, embellisher, and so on. This is the one that we all can't live without.

Pure entertainment value in this type of person. I love the internet and that we have a way to check things out. My personal stepdad was a fighter pilot and war hero with secret missions. Oh, how the bar hoppers ate that up, to no end. Then to find out he was an aircraft mechanic on those same planes, only to hear and live the dreams of others. These people are alive and well, ready to share tales of disbelief with us. The sad thing is that the truth will almost always catch up in the end. You may be able to hide *from* the truth but you can't hide the truth, not forever anyway. Hopefully you are not a victim of this scenario.

Pepe le Pew: A great memory for me in my hunt for a life partner was watching the infamous Pepe le Pew. This sly skunk was in love with the elusive and stunning cat. He would change how he looked and smelled to get close enough to the dream of his imagination. I have a friend who married one of these chamelions. Within a week of signing the papers, the true motives and behavior began to settle in. In the end, a skunk is still a skunk, and unless you can put up with the stink, step back and get a breath of fresh air.

Quiet Ones Wow, the experience is kind of like the hater, but more like a missile in your face. I love this relationship the most on the receiver, because they agree with everything that is fun and dear to you. Forget that they have a voice of their own and pimp them into your world, where they will live for an uncharted time. There may be a slight chance that you can negotite detante and diffuse the missile before the cold war settles into place.

Sloppy Seconds: Do they (almost) constantly talk about their ex or how they are going to win them back again? This may be a clue that you are involved in a rebound relationship. Get your parachute ready. There is a high probability that you may be dumped.

The Stockholm Syndrome: Applies to anyone who has been coerced, abducted, or held hostage in a relationship. If the mental abuse is not enough, just for fun add black and blue marks, circles under the eyes, and interesting explanations about how that bone got broken. Note the peculiar tendency to jump whenever a short, angry word is uttered. With proper Pavlovian conditioning you can release this type into the world and they will come back again and again. This one definitely needs professional help.

Thirty-day Gym Membership: We strive to keep up with the latest membership knowing that it can only last long enough to break a sweat. I find that with our generation of young, blending with the middle and older generations, we are getting into some complicated workouts. Do you ride the treadmill, fake walk the track, do the free weights, just for the little burst that it takes to conquer the sweat? Because all you must do is push the stop button, get a sprained ankle, or pull a muscle. Suddenly the monotonous bike ride breaks apart because it was not planned and the journey now goes up and down the perilous mountains. In my opinion, if we look at our membership as a long-term contract we might actually get somewhere and accomplish a great enjoyment that has never been felt before. Instead of looking at what the other person is going to do for you, do it for yourself first and then share the experience. It's is a better bang for the buck instead of paying every month for a few days a week or less.

Validate My Parking: Like Webster, there are two definitions here. (1) One who moves in or otherwise occupies space with the purpose of needing someone to validate their life every second of every day. (2) A casual shopper expecting something free, as in, *I bought into your crap, now validate my parking*.

Victim: Who came up with this role in life? Why is it written into my script of day-to-day living? This person can manipulate a situation like no other but loves to share that their life hasn't been like a box of chocolates. If they were robbed, you will be too, especially if you stay in this mode. You're sure to find more victims on your path.

How many of these types have you encountered or perhaps even observed in other people's relationships? Have you ever been trapped by one or another of them? Sometimes the best path to self improvement leads away from the present environment. This can be a hard but necessary choice. If at first you don't succeed, try, try again and don't give up on yourself. Above all, LEARN from your mistakes and life will definitely get easier.

How do you define yourself? What do you want to be in life? What do you project? Pick your character in life carefully. Do you want to be a jerk, a nice person, gay but straight person, biker dude, cowboy or whatever life lets you be (without breaking the law of course)?

To make it simple, start from a place in your past that you find comfortable to understand. Where are you from? How did you live and grow up? It's like filling out a job application for yourself.

You might think of this as your travel guide key, like the legend on a map. This is your Journey, whether alone or with a best friend that you might marry or just be with to share those sought after good memories. I'm talking about the ones we hold dear and remember in the golden years, hanging out with, hopefully, friends and family.

These memories are forever, so put a good foot

forward and don’t stub your toe or break an ankle tripping over the potholes life puts in your path. You don’t plant a seed in the Sahara desert expecting something to grow without water. Find the right environment with the right person and you both will thrive.

It's fun to look at yourself and laugh occasionally, but in all seriousness, try not to fall into the hands of an incompatible or difficult partner. Therapists, bartenders, and friends will all tell you to run from a toxic relationship. Consider this advice seriously if it comes from more than a few people. They are likely seeing *something* from their perspective that you may not see.

It is easy to assume that when seeking a long-term relationship, you should find someone who shares your common interests. Nothing could be further from the truth. Let me share with you personal observations from three couples who I know.

Margo and Rob Married over 45 years. Despite being two opposites, they are BEST FRIENDS.
Rob: Professor Hobbies: Books/movies
Margo: Nurse Hobbies: remodeling
Common interests: They go to breakfast every Saturday morning at 6am and talk about their week and what they did. Not fixing any problems, just listening and conversation.
Kids: they put everything towards this deal. As an only child with these parents, he is making out quite well.

Lana and Jack Married over 43 years plus BEST FRIENDS. They are two opposites.
Jack: Garbage business owner Hobbies: guns/hunting
Lana: Cosmetologist Hobbies: sewing
Common interests: They travel on days off, horse-riding, and having friends come over.
Kids: The kids were opposites: one took over the business and the other followed mom as a cosmetologist.

Bob and Meredith Married 39 years plus BEST FRIENDS. They are two opposites.
Bob: Machinist Hobbies: carving and fishing
Meredith: CEO Secretary Hobbies: fishing and photography
Common interests: They go camping and fishing together all summer and she helps run her daughter's store, while he carves and makes flies.
Kids: two girls, opposites, one a career mom and the other mom's project and co-business owner. One married and the other probably never will marry.

A subject that is important to know: Make sure you have or learn a strong escape instinct. If your memory sucks, if fear has struck you immobile, or if you keep justifying bad behaviors to not be alone, keep a diary. Why do we need this? Because a journal becomes a record of our life. Forgetting the past is easy, except when it's written down. Key points to notice: are you cornered often, feel captured, or even herded into a situation you are not comfortable with? Write about your environment. You can reflect on it and observe whether it changes slowly or immediately.

If you find yourself in a position where you continually ask yourself “What's wrong with me?”, and it happens again and again, a journal will help provide the answers. Otherwise, change your environment. Maybe join a club or organization that interests you so you can meet up with similar people that would better fit your lifestyle and needs.

Watch what you consume. We are under the constant assault of the media, vying for our attention and our money. You may laugh at the dysfunctional characters you see, but what are you gaining? Do you really want to associate with these dysfunctional characters, let alone adopt their habits? If you sit at home and consume too much television, guzzling it like free beer, you're bound to get drunk and dizzy. The fact is, real life can be more fun and interactive.

Next subject. The Personal Bubble is something we all have. Is it big or small? Bubble Boys are popular. Hollywood made a movie about *The Boy in the Bubble*. The show *Northern Exposure* featured a bubble boy one season. One of my favorite *Seinfeld* episodes was about a boy they visited who lived in a bubble. People who live in bubbles that are tight never feel the real world, only what they can imagine to be real.

In all my years of reflecting on my life and all the interactions with others, I have found that we have a specific type of bubble around us. What I mean is this: we may have had a traumatic something happen to one of our three main senses. The outcome of that is a certain amount of space that we deem our special distance with others. Some of us carry a briefcase full of sizes with them along with the ability to switch between them as they see fit.

A bubble that is small and thick might come from divorce, being destitute and homeless, an alcoholic, touched as a kid; the list of bad crap that happens to us is endless. But then, most of us get up in the morning and start the day with at least a little bit of constructive attitude. We manage to somehow accomplish something every day to enrich our future for better or worse, but hopefully for better. This is true self improvement.

A bubble that is large has tons of space for everyone. You had a great life or had a great example in life. You like to hug and laugh with everyone. You possibly like to go to festivals, raves, or big concerts. Church may be a big part of your life, or some other form of shared fellowship. You somehow connect with people in joyful ways.

Whatever your bubble or however big, we can all learn to have a happy bubble, even if it's small. This is a book of discovery. Open your mind to your own heart and imagination and focus less on what we take in and absorb from our surroundings.

Do you look at where you live as your bubble? Sadly, there are those among us who live in a one room bubble. I know people that haven’t left a house or apartment for four, eight, maybe ten years. Mobility may be part of the problem, or some other problem that makes us go into isolation. Then again, the good die young and the rest of us get old and feeble. Which brings up another point. Why wait until you're old to forget your past? You can't do much about it except apologize and ask for forgiveness from anyone you may have injured. This is actually a good activity, as any twelve stepper will tell you.

What you get in life is what you put into it. It's like making a cake, if you don't add all the ingredients and follow the instructions, that cake is going to taste nasty. Use quality ingredients and try not to change what tastes good and it will remain consistent.

Things to Consider

List five things you believe make a successful relationship:

1.

2

3.

4.

5.

Write down what menu items you want in a partner:

Eye Color:

Hair Color:

Body Type:

Personality:

Package:

Kids:

In-Laws:

Race:

Religion:

Political Party or Beliefs:

Job/Type of Work:

Abilities:

Hobbies:

Vegan, meateater, special dietary requirements:

Education:

Pets:

Smoker:

Sexual preference:

Other:

Turnoffs:

Deal Breakers:

Chapter 3
The Perfect Marriage

Life is nothing but adjustments.

Ron Proebstl

Before we go any further let me state, there is no perfect marriage. What works for one couple can be a disaster for another. I have observed many marriages that do not fit any mold or set of rules. Somehow and someway, they last for years and are successful and vibrant.

As part of my research, I asked women how they defined “a good catch”. No, hung like a horse was not the number one answer (although it did come up). Instead, the terms financially supportive, educated, self motivated, and good job ranked at the top. Things like security and religious beliefs were in the middle. In-laws didn't really matter.

What do women expect in a marriage? What can make a marriage endure? Compatibility is one thing, but there are different levels of compatibility. Anyone that has been stuck in the "friend zone" knows that they may be compatible as friends, but might never be considered "marriage material."

Men basically want the same thing. A secure relationship with a caring partner. True, they tend to dominate a relationship, but this is where compromise and honest communication come in.

I had a friend tell me about something her live-in boyfriend did that irritated her to no end. Every morning he would shave and brush his teeth, leaving a mess in the bathroom sink. Upon seeing it, she would seethe, take a towel, and wipe out the sink.

"Did you ever tell him about it or about your feelings?" I asked.

"No," she said. "I thought it would topple the relationship."

This may have been true, although I would question the stregnth of any relationship that would fall apart over something as simple as this. Communication and compromise would have definately made life easier. Why hold something in, especially if it is a sore point. My point in telling this story is: men are not mind readers. Most of us are clueless, but women already know that. Again, decide whether the anxiety of holding something in outweighs the fear of sharing it, and act accordingly.

We have been talking about a traditional marriage, but gender roles are irrelevant. If you don't accept that, and you're still living in the fifties, wake up. When something rubs against your grain, it's a message to yourself. There's something for you to learn there. The answer might be found in the higher principles of love, compassion, understanding, and forgiveness (especially forgiveness for yourself). Personally, I find it hard to deny anyone the right to be whoever they want to be, although I don't agree with myself when it comes to criminals and psychopaths.

A word about open marriages, sado masochists, polyamorous people, kings and queens and everything in between: that's all fine and well if that's what you want in a marriage, as long as you both agree to it. That is the key to any successful marriage. Anything goes, as long as you both agree to it. And the hell with what in-laws and everyone else thinks or says. It's your marriage, not theirs.

The Seven Day Marriage will work no matter what your arrangement. It's about finding out you are best friends and building a life together. I haven't tested it on parties of four or more. Two is complicated enough for me.

Paying attention to your partner is important. A compliment goes a long way, so don't overdo it. It begins to sound less than genuine. Watch the inflection in your voice and make it honest. I find it amazing that, even with good communication, a message can get garbled. I have a pat answer to the question “How do I look?” It's usually the same. “Pretty good.” I've noticed that even though the words are the same, they come out differently, sometimes sounding like “WOW” and other times like “Meh.” It seems we put emotion behind our words whether we want to or not.

Other traits that we sometimes don’t even think about as important. How does the other person project themselves? Observe them, as well as yourself, and you will find clues about your deeper feelings. Here are a few things to look for:

Relaxed: Do they appear to be comfortable, non-stressed in conversation, you get the idea.

Stretching: Are they constantly looking around as if half-interested in what you’re selling?

Yawning: Try not to be rude to someone that needs more oxygen to the brain. Your space might be too small to share.

Alert: Stiff, but at your attention, semi-relaxed, and into getting to know you.

Tense: Stiff also, but just shy to the touch and might smell and look good, so definitely worth a shot so... Don't over-think or justify it away unless they are definitely not your type.

Fearful: You can't be too trustful these days with all the weirdos out there. Slow and careful can be rewarding, otherwise you wonder what did I adopt? Hopefully you didn't rush in and share your habitat or get married!

I have three simple rules for a successful marriage: No stealing. No secrets. No lies.

All this food for thought is great, and it's the kind of stuff you'd expect to find in a self-help book. The kind of stuff I hate. But this is a self-improvement book and I need to mention it. It was important on my journey, maybe it will be helpful on yours.

Before you get married, take a serious look at yourself. Let's start with something simple. Why do you want a serious partnership like marriage? Here are a few reasons why people want to get married. How many apply to you?

	They're rich. I'll never have to work again!
	I want children and a family
	My parents want me to find someone and get married
	I'm not getting any younger.
	I want someone to care for
	Oops, the condom broke
	I can't get them to move out, why not marry them?
	I like their dog
	I want to take care of their kids. They need me
	I think I'll be happier married
	I'm tired of working
	We go to the same church. It's a match made in heaven
	There are Government benefits to being married
	I can't picture my life without this person
	My stuff needs fixing and they're a good handyman
	People learn to love through close relationships
	I'm lonely. It's boring being alone
	We've been dating long enough. Where else is this heading?
	I always wanted a big wedding with caterers, fancy clothes, and all the attention
	It's the only way to put my best friend on the company health plan
	I'm being coerced and blackmailed into marriage
	I feel safe with this person and I need someone to protect me
	It's the right thing to do
	She's pregnant with another person's child. She needs my support. I'll rescue her by proposing marriage.
	Having the right partner can make life easier
	I need someone to be with me and validate my life

	I want my citizenship
	They are old and will die soon and I will inherit everything
	The dowry includes a house/boat/car/whatever
	My life would be incomplete without you
	All my friends are married now
	I'm ready for the challenge of marriage
	I need someone to take care of me and do my laundry
	I tried single. I always wondered what marriage was like
	I'm ready to settle down
	They are a good catch
	Everybody needs a training marriage. My second or third will be great
	I want to be with someone when I'm old
	My younger sister / brother just got married
	I'm divorced or widowed and need someone to fill the void
	I lose the trust fund if I don't get married by the time I'm thirty
	So I can get a makeover and wear the white dress
	Grandma won't die happy if I'm still single
	I need a partner to look good with at church and company parties
	We're doing it for the children
	I'm afraid to be alone
	Why not get married?
	I want someone who'll appreciate me
	My parents were married and had kids by this age
	The invitations have already been mailed. I can't back out now
	I found my life partner and soul mate. My search is over
	Two can live cheaper than one, and I get a tax break!
	We're sexually compatible
	Because a marital partner cannot be forced to testify against you in a

	court of law.
	I sear it's going to be easy
	I can commit my life to a single individual
	They seem to put up with me and my quirky ways
	I'm in love

Let's look a little closer at that last one. No matter what you think or how much you plan, love seems to trump all. Do you do what your heart says, or do you think things through? A little of both may make a balanced approach, but this is all the more reason for the Seven Day Marriage. As Merlin says to Arthur in *Camelot*: “Thinking helps in everything but love. Love is sort of like a holiday, so thinking can rest.”

Don't be disappointed if things don't work out. The Love Story that ends is simple and encompasses (1) What you did, (2) What they did, and (3) What everyone saw. Listen to the debriefing you get from friends and relatives. It may help to tip your heart one way or another. Look at it as a life lesson. Scientists learn from their failures as much as from success. So can you.

Quit putting the cherry on top. So, you didn't win

the race! Again, go back to that comfortable place. Think about where you are from, how you lived and who you grew up with. Don't think that just because someone is together with someone else, it doesn't mean they are happy or can get out of a crappy relationship. We need to learn from positive examples in our world and understand where we might need to go in life.

Trust is that indescribable quality that makes people open up to each other. Cultivating trust is like building your house on solid rock instead of sand. Trust is a big part of marriage, of any partnership. It is a statement that says: my partner will catch me when I fall backwards.

A word about trust: Once it is broken, it is very hard to repair. It can depend on the degree of the transgression. Some things might be easy to fix, like a bounced check or a missed appointment. Something like a love affair might take longer. Just saying "I'm sorry" may not be enough. Actions speak louder than words, and they must be consistent otherwise the message is muddled. To rebuild the trust, walk carefully. Accept that a mistake was made. It is an opportunity to practice forgiveness, understanding, and compassion.

There are questions at the end of this chapter to help you. Fill them out before you start the Seven Day Marriage. Pull what you know about yourself out of the deep recesses of your mind and put it down on paper where it is tangible. Start a journal dedicated to your self. Marriage can merge two people into one. Your thoughts will help you better track your progress. You can evaluate where you've been, what is important to you, and where you are headed.

This journey begins with YOU!

Things to consider

How do you feel about children?

☐ *I have no children*

☐ *I have ____ from a prior relationship.*

☐ *I do not want children. (Please elaborate):*

How about pets?

☐ *I don't like pets*

☐ *I have no pets*

☐ *I have these pets*

_____ *dog(s)* _____ *cat(s)* ____ *rabbit(s)*

_____ *fish* _____ *snake(s)* ____ *bird(s)*

_____

_____

Residence:

☐ *We move in together at my place.*

☐ *Your place.*

☐ *Let's find a new place together.*

Finances:

☐ *We get a joint bank account.*

☐ *We both work, let's keep separate accounts.*

☐ *I have money. I will take care of you.*

☐ *What's mine is mine, what's yours is ours.*

☐ *I can cover these expenses*

____

____

____

Expectations

What expectations do you have of me?

☐ *cook*

☐ *general housework and cleaning*

☐ *clean the bathroom*

☐ *take out the garbage*

☐ *household repairs*

☐ *car repairs*

☐ *grocery shopping*

☐ *dishwashing*

☐ *make the bed in the morning*

☐ *yard work*

☐ *pay bills*

☐ *pay ______% of the rent*

☐ *Leave the toilet seat down* ☐ *or up*

☐ *Dog walking/pet care*

☐ *Laundry*

☐ *We hire a maid*

☐ *One of us stays home while the other works*

☐ ______________________________

☐ ______________________________

☐ ______________________________

You can make some notes for yourself in the space below. Gather your thoughts. They are a roadmap towards a successful marriage. Remember, you are exploring life with your Best Friend!

Chapter 4

You're the Same Person You've Always Been

You can change the label on the album,
but the record still plays the same tune.
Break the record!

- J. Hutchins

Psychologists and sociologists will tell you that by the time we are five, our personality and habits are pretty well set. What we see and take in when we are young influences our whole life. A friend of mine hated girls when he was young. He now hates women. Another was always interested in toys that built things like Lincoln Logs and Erector Sets. He's a successful engineer now. Bullies become sadists; do the sneaky ones become politicians? I don't know but I have a list that goes on and on.

The point is, you have to become comfortable with yourself. Before you think about spending the rest of your life with someone else, see how comfortable you are living with yourself. There's the real personality that you will be living with forever. Better start the road to happiness, self improvement, and contentment with some good old fashioned introspection.

Some partners get married thinking that they will be able to change the one they married. I've seen it happen in some rare cases, but usually the person does not change. Change seems to occur in a very dramatic way for us as individuals. Marriage is certainly a life changing event. A marriage of equals, between Best Friends who respect each other, has the best chances for success.

There is an old joke: How many psychiatrists does it take to change a light bulb? Only one, but the light bulb has to really want to change.

There is a core belief deep inside us that shapes who we are. It starts with thoughts that emerge from deep within your brain. We are what we believe we are. This is the key to changing your programming. You must learn to think differently. Not so much differently, but perhaps looking at yourself from another angle. The more ways you look at something, the better your perspective. This leads to more effective life decisions.

Much of our information on how to act comes from the environment around us. Television, movies, books (even ones like this), social media, news feeds, our friends and lovers. We process that information, react to it, and somehow synthesize it, integrating it into something we call our "self".

Does this self act consistently? This is the first thing you might ask. Do you make the same choices again and again? How do you analyze and make these choices? Are they good choices or bad choices? Impulsive or well thought through? How about your choices in a partner?

The desire to change can also be a strong force. The most dramatic I have seen I might call Divine Intervention. It's a common theme in literature and popular movies. The villain, through some introspective mechanism, looks deep into their soul and has a transformation. Darth Vader, Eastwood in *Unforgiven*, *The Magnificent Seven*, and my favorite: Bogart as Rick in *Casablanca*. We love stories where the bad guy turns good. Then they either die or the movie ends. This leaves the open question; do they ever revert to their old behaviors?

I've seen people accept Jesus in church, walk up to the alter and be saved. Even that does not seem to change core beliefs except in a rare few instances. After a while, the old habits emerge. But if there is anything that can instantaneously change a person, it is Divine Intervention followed up with a moral code that reinforces the change. If you want change, take a tip from Alcoholics Anonymous. The first tenet of any good twelve step program starts with accept you are powerless over (whatever) followed by ask your higher power to change (whatever). Once again I emphasize that this change is followed up by a strong moral code.

So there you go! Change is possible. How does that work in a marriage? I call it the best friend code. Think about your past for a moment. Think about all the silly things you did with your best friend. Adventures and antics that seem to be the things you never forget. Now think about your marriage and your partner. Are the memories the same? Are the antics and adventures ones you shared with your partner? Congratulations, you married your best friend.

Any marriage that lasts twenty years or more is most often between best friends. I married my best friend. If you're not with your best friend, then why are you wasting your time and theirs?

Some people crave the drama. I know a couple that fought a lot. I got embarrassed when I visited them. Sometimes I noticed damaged furniture, missing knick-knacks, and mysterious holes in the wall. This behavior became a ritual for them, all because they wanted the "kiss and make up" experience. A little yin, a little yang, keeps the excitement going, at least for them. Unfortunately, the ride got tired for one or both of them and the marriage ended miserably. I guess it wasn't cute anymore.

I was living with my brother while he was working on his thesis. Observing his research and studying beside him, I came up with the Honeymoon Cycle. Here's how it works. You get married and have the honeymoon. For some, this phase never ends. There may be bumps in the road along the way, but hey, that's life. This is another moment when you realize you married your best friend. You respect each other, communicate, and share your choices. For others, they fall into the Honeymoon Cycle.

It starts with the realization that the honeymoon is over. Something happens, something you don't like. Socks on the floor, "bad" sleep habits, they never cook, and *you expect me to do what?* Now we move into the next phase, building resentment. This phase is full of judgment, bad memories, and underlying emotions that build like a volcano. You start to hold on to the bad things, looking for them to reoccur. *There's those socks on the floor again. Don't they see how this is driving me nuts?*

Unless you're a mind reader, there is usually no communication in this phase. Best friends usually never let it get to this point. They practice compromise and communication, like all best friends do. Remember when you were a kid? Your best friend wanted to play ball but you wanted to go on a walk somewhere. What did you do? Compromise.

The second basis for a strong friendship is communication. Have you ever had a partner that seethed with resentment, given you the silent treatment, or cut you off completely? Were you expected to develop mind reading and psychic skills that would rival *The Great Kreskin*? It's likely there was something between you and your partner that you didn't talk about. If you didn't speak up for what you want, for whatever reason, then you only have yourself to blame. Don't try to play the victim, it's not an act anyone likes to see. Go back to basics and communicate.

I have a relative that I questioned about marriage. His second marriage was his best. He said they were like best friends, sharing life's adventures, doing things together, and telling each other everything including the deep secrets buried in our souls. A little more probing and I discovered he did not have the same, best friend relationship with his first wife. He came home from the office at times, unable to discuss what was on his mind. There were secrets, more and more of them as time went on. Things that were withheld and could not be shared, for whatever reason. This is a sure sign you did not marry your best friend.

So no compromise, no communication? Are you ready to move forward into the next phase of the Honeymoon Cycle. The resentment has built, seething and boiling until it is ready to erupt as sure as Old Faithful. There is an ancient Chinese saying: To suppress something is to give it great force. While these forces are building, so do the ideas in your head about what you're going to do. What follows is the justification for whatever actions are under consideration. The justification builds as options are explored, in thought at first, until the Honeymoon Cycle rolls into the next phase. What you actually do.

Now something really happens. An affair, gambling, stopping at the bar on the way home, turning to friends, something that just brings out what I call the scream for help. Sometimes it is too late and the action is unforgivable. The Honeymoon Cycle is broken and so is the marriage. Otherwise we move on to the last phase. Everything is on the table. Where we go from here? Do we make up, or do we move on? How long does it take to make that decision? A day? A week? Six months? How long will your Honeymoon Cycle last?

Until it starts again. The only way out is compromise and communication, especially if you want to stay best friends.

There are some changes that are out of our control. I know more than a few women who would have liked to avoid menopause. And to be fair, guys go through the same thing, we just call it a mid-life crisis. These are chemical changes to our bodies as we grow older. Sex usually fades without the help of those "male enhancement drugs" or a good dose of stabilizing hormones. What makes a marriage survive something like this? You have to have the other fundamentals in place.

My grandfather once told me he overheard women talking about menopause at work. "I lost my sex drive," he heard one woman say. "It's just not fair to him." They were best friends, willing to sacrifice, thinking of the other person. Talking things over with a friend before springing it on a partner can help explore many perspectives. In the end, your friend can help you find the right words to bridge a difficult discussion with your partner.

I love the soap operas for that reason. Someone has an affair or comes out as gay or does something else dramatic. You get to see all the characters react to it, hear all kinds of perspectives. Sometimes you'll hear a character you identify with say something totally unexpected and it triggers a new train of thought in your brain. This is an example of how television can be educational and constructive. You just have to live through the commercials or buy the premium experience from the network website. For the sake of brevity, I will refrain from any comments on the many marriages of Erica Kane.

I mentioned Lorena Bobbit before. Did you do your homework and look her up? Let's talk about John Bobbit, her husband. To start with, they found his manhood on the lawn and reattached it. He became a big porn star and later a preacher, dramatic changes by any standard. Change is the evidence we leave behind on our journey. How you react to the change in your life determines the next cycle of your existence. Constructive self criticism and effective action can trigger change in the direction you truly want to go. And a best friend can help you get there.

So, do you want a perfect partner that does this, this, and *this*? Yes, we may get married for such things as love, sex, and money. I don't think anyone gets married for compromise. It's more like something learned after marriage. After all, how can anyone help being themselves?

One path to self improvement can be to allow the change that marriage brings. Fear sometimes stops us from making this change. Perhaps it is the fear of losing your "self". Talk about your fears, about what changes you would like to make, what support you need, and what you know needs improvement, but aren't quite ready to tackle. If you trust your partner, if you married your best friend, if you communicate honestly, then you have nothing to lose.

Remember, there is a big difference between what you do and who you are. If you want to live happy, be who you are, but don't just be a partner, be a best friend. And keep this in mind: the light bulb really has to want to change.

Food for thought

If you had a magic wand and could change anything, what would it be? Is it anything you could share with your partner? Do you think they could help you with this change?

TRIGGERS

A trigger is something that sets you off. It could be something as simple as an unwashed sink full of dishes, a spoken phrase or word, an emotional outburst, a smell, even a place or an event. These triggers are often based on some past trauma. They can be doorways into the subconscious when brought to light and explored. Confronting them boldly can open the path to self discovery and free you from these behaviors. Either way, your partner deserves to know your triggers, that way they can avoid them when they unexpectedly come up and help you get over them when they accidentally do.

List some of your "triggers".

In the space remaining, list anything else you want your partner to know about. Medical conditions, sensitivities, hobbies, musical abilities, addictions, kinks, anything!

Chapter 5

Why and What is the Seven Day Marriage?

> *Even the longest journey of a thousand miles begins with a single step.*
>
> Lao Tzu, *The Tao Te Ching*

If you think you are ready to get married, invest your life in another human being, or undertake anything that requires a true understanding, consider the Seven Day Marriage before you get into a situation that could have been avoided. You can even apply this to a partnership for a business. It doesn't matter what your sexual orientation is, it still works. It even works if you're considering being roommates for an extended period of time. I want you to explore the possibilities, so here's what to do:

First, plan a 7-day trip. Here are the rules:

It must be one house, apartment, hotel room, tent, RV, whatever, but together for everything. Eating, sleeping, and all activities in between. Well, bathroom privacy accepted. But no sneaking around, no secret phone calls, no outside interference.

Most important: only the potential partners are to be involved in this journey. No animals, kids, no in-laws, friends, no one else. They are distractions!

I never said Sex must be any part of this.

Have fun in whatever you are going to do, whether it is camping, a train ride with stops, vacation in Hawaii, a cruise, a house to do business in and set up a partnership, hopefully you get the idea here.

My Aunt and Uncle, one a therapist, the other a school administrator, have over fifty strong years together. They challenge you to a Seven Day Camping Trip. They call it their EXTREME Seven Day Marriage. Pooping in the woods together is part of the plan. Aww, now that's sharing.

What? You don't feel creative enough to come up with events together? Both of you write down things on pieces of paper and put them in a hat. Draw two every day and go for it. Still at a loss? Try some of my favorite suggestions:

Go to a park or someplace with a table. Sit opposite each other and stare at each other's face. You'll be looking at that mug the rest of your life. Better get used to it now.

Sit and model for each other as you draw a picture of your potential mate.

Play Truth or Dare. This is how we learned about our friends when we were young and how we subtly revealed ourselves through clever dares. Other simple, revealing games include Cards Against Humanity, Strip Poker, Chess, Jeopardy, staring contests, The Newlywed Game, Two

Truths and a Lie, Would You Rather, or even Doctor, my favorite when I was young. Ever play "House" when you were a kid? If you played it now, what would your role be? Still stumped for games. Make up your own, if they are not cruel (unless you like that sort of thing).

Pack a lunch and have a picnic. One or the other serves and plays the caregiver. Then take turns. Go fishing. Take a wine tour. Go to an amusement park. Author event. Time share presentation. Gym. Just drive around looking at scenery, houses, buildings, whatever.

For pure fun, try games like Twister, bowling, ping pong, touch football, or even a three-legged race against nobody. If anything, that will show how well you can work together.

You may be good at certain things but stay away from games like belching contests and fart wars. Also, to avoid: Beer Pong, Daredevil, Slap, and Stick Quiz. What? Never heard of Stick Quiz? You get asked a question and if you get it wrong, you get hit with a stick. It was a game we played in the old, tough neighborhood I grew up in.

There are worksheets and scorekeeping tools in the workbook to help you track events and record the memories. If you keep a diary or a journal, so much the better. The material is meant to help you track, evaluate, and process the days as they pass.

SPOILER ALERT

The following pages are full of stories, observations, and other things I have learned from many Seven Day Marriage experiences, including my own. Since every experience is unique, these stories may not be what's in store for you. It may be better to start each day with a blank slate and follow it up at night by sharing workbooks.

However, if you're having trouble processing what's happening, these stories may help bring things into perspective. The great thing about being human is we can learn from other people's experience. So, read on if you want, just be aware that your experience may not be the same as those depicted in the rest of this chapter. In fact, we'd love to hear about your experience. And no matter how it turns out, good luck and have fun.

Day 1

The first day of marriage.

Last night you travelled and are a bit tired or maybe you're the rise and shine type. Are you up alone, on your third cup of coffee and still waiting? If you didn't know this before you tied the knot and signed on the dotted line. Guess what? You do now!!!

It's okay, because whatever happens, hopefully they are just as beautiful in the morning as you are. If this is your first marriage, you are going to either pull out your skills or start packing your bags for the end of this journey.

This is the easy way to start the day. Say "Good Morning, afternoon, or evening my love," depending on when you get up after you arrive on your new adventure. We must *Hear* in order to feed our brain and decide whether we want *I love you* or *I want to put up with your crap every day*.

You chose to get to this point, so play the game, because this is life as we know it. We make each day what we want it to be. If you are reading this and think this is not important, you might be a KAREN!

But know that this is the rest of your awesome life together and I can't wait to make memories that will be cerished.

I believe on day one you are on your best behavior because if it ends up being your fault, we know what happens next. Enjoy everything you do together whether it is hiking, TMI, eating foods you like, public displays of affection, or compromising. Be who you were before you signed on the dotted line and committed to the new life that you will share. It's not just your life anymore. This day can really be a psychological nightmare for some because they think that their identity might get swayed, changed, or even forgotten. Put the pen away and make memories. Start the new person you want to be, which was the same person you were last week, unless you were in the doghouse.

Don't forget to fill out your daily worksheets. Discuss the results openly if you wish.

Day 2

On with the adventure!

Wow, did they just sleep in, or did they naturally wake up in a super bitchy mood again. Or was it, holy crap! How many times a night do you have to pee, or roll over. Some good old favorites are: the blanket or bed hog, sweat all night, the roar and snore, drooly, sleep naked, sleepwalk, and sorry I talk in my sleep. I had a partner who would randomly interrupt my sleep saying, “I'm here. I'm bored. Wake up and play with me.” It was cute for a while, but it wore out quickly.

Start with “Good morning my Love” again, and everyday whether together or not. We need to hear positive and affirming statements of togetherness and it can make the bond so much stronger, especially for some people. This connection can be more powerful than our touch connection. With that note, if you are not touching each other in a loving way, holding hands, rubbing their back or feet after a long day of walking, or speaking kindly to each other, this is your day two challenge. Watch your partner's style and behaviors for clues on how they treat you. You might want to see if this is something you can deal with, THE REST OF YOUR LIFE!

Do something spontaneous this day, and have the other person plan it, unless you are absolutely no good at it and you both agree the event is not allowed. COMPROMISE. I guess this word is not used much anymore since Burger King's "Have it your Way" slogan came out. There is also something known as the win-win scenario, as imaginary and elusive as that may be. I believe compromise is something we did when we were little kids and you and your best friend probably hung out most of the summer and sometimes your friendship ended because you never wanted to do what they wanted to do. I do believe having other best friends as you grow up can compromise your current one. But if that's the case, which best friend do you want to know and make memories with the rest of your life?

Day 3
The Show must go on!

This is where reality and fantasy start to make sense and blend together to give us the understanding that our minds often trick us into believing. What I mean is, this is the third day of the rest of your life unless you are in the percentage of our culture that doesn't want change. You can continue to use people to your benefit and make sure you are the "Happy One", believing in the unwritten rule that it is a game about whoever wins and with how much.

Push yourself, be daring and explore each other like you were lost continents. Build trust, one truth or one secret at a time. It's the present moment that counts. I love this day because you get to find out pretty much how daily life and struggles are going to be. This is where the questions and conversation can really get good as two people open and share the thoughts and ideas of their future together.

Day 4
Approaching the moment of truth

Did you say “Good morning my Love” again and again everyday whether together or not? Say it with meaning if you want to have a long and happy journey in life.

OR

You either gave up at this point and you’re just enjoying the vacation with a friend but not your soul mate. You might feel that this is just a fling, doomed for the one year annulment, three year nightmare, more of the same, or the infamous seven year ditch!

If this is not you, then awesome sauce and start the day like it was your last dying day. Celebrate how we made it past this day. If this is your first journey and are still in love, then I believe nothing will come between two soulmates that are best friends. I hope that you are not killing each other or planning a quick death. Do yourself a favor and save the money and heartaches for another journey.

If this day brings those subtle memories of the last few days to light, it can be like fingers on a chalkboard, lingering vomit in your mouth, or the clouded brain of nowhere. If this is so, we must be honest and end the contract. This is the day breaker and can save money on the wedding of a lifetime for the one that can get through the Seven Day Marriage. So be honest, speak up and clear up a situation that would fester and pop, and find out if it is something that can be discussed and saved with COMPROMISE!!!

Day 5

Over the Hump or in the Dump

Great day, because you are almost there. Today you are going to find all the little endearments that will be great memories forever.

If it becomes a day of misery, rethink what you are about to do. Maybe life together is too much to ask in this situation. You can end it now, amicably and without the help of a lawyer.

Don't forget what we need to do every morning and say, "Good morning my Love," whether you must wake them up or not, because it could be the last time you say I love you and then something bad happens and we don't get closure if it does.

Today I want you to tell the other person something personal about yourself that you need to get off your chest or clear in your mind. I had to tell my soul mate about being molested at a young age. Confess something that makes you feel vulnerable. This fosters trust. Talk about your problem with drugs they don’t know about, or a gambling addiction, or your kinky habits. It's easier to learn about it now rather than after the wedding.

My mother received very little sex education in her day. Her mother never said anything. On her wedding night, she was shocked at what my father expected her to do. Let there be no surprises. Get it out in the open.

I know, you think you know everything about this person, and if you found out it wouldn’t be a big deal, but you’re dead wrong. Keeping a secret that doesn’t affect someone else is a secret. Take that to your grave as it won't give anyone but you an understanding. I knew a friend that found out later his wife had genital herpes, and boy did that almost ruin a friendship and a $40,000 wedding that daddy just sprung for.

Are we getting the point yet? This is a contract for life, not just a car loan on something that, if not well maintained, is just going to break down and then all you want to do or think about is the new model that is available. I wish that someone had told me some of these things before being married four times!

Then there's all the crappy self-help books I read, counseling, and even a three day Christian based Marriage Encounters was not going to save me. All because I didn't know I could just take a seven day vacation with the person that I was going to stay with, building a long lasting-until we die type marriage.

I remember having to go to a mandatory court ordered parent divorce seminar to get it finalized because we had kids. I don't know if this is still mandatory, but one of the points and participation we all did was to answer this question: "More than half of you in this auditorium will get remarried in one year or close to it. Raise your hand if this is not you." I did and then crap I was married in 10 months, because I thought I was smarter than them. I was also divorced in less than a year because when we went on our honeymoon and then a vacation three months later, I wanted to run away and eventually did a few months after that.

All we ask is you be honest with yourself and your potential mate. Discuss things openly, communicate clearly while keeping emotions in check, and compromise if that is what is desired.

Day 6
What Did I Say?

Stop, you had a fight or argument, and you are reverting like it was day 3 right before you knew everything that was going to happen. Put the pen down and remember that this is my Best Friend, that this stuff doesn't matter squat until we sign on the dotted line with our real names and make it all official. So instead, we forgot the words like compromise, trying to justify behaviors, thinking about those skeletons in the closet that are trying to get some air, anything legit because they say our imagination can always get the best of us. Don't just guess what someone is thinking, ask. Remember one thing this week: unless we change something in our lives on purpose or because the universe changes it for us, this is the same person you get to experience all this with.

Day 7
Finish Line in Sight

You made it! You still get to decide if all the things you thought that mattered, still matter. You didn't just spend $30K on the wedding and a lavish honeymoon that went south on day two of seven and now you must spend more money, more time, and deal with a lot of crap because you rushed into a life with no regard for yourself or the other person. So, do society a favor and the next generation to come. Create a smoother road like in the song John Lennon wanted all of us to IMAGINE.

Complete the day 7 questionnaire and fill out the exit materials. Enjoy life, whether it worked out or not. You still came out ahead.

Chapter 6

Other Things to Think About

Words are, in my not-so-humble opinion, our most inexhaustable source of magic. Capable of both inflicting injury, and remedying it.

Dumbledore in *Harry Potter and the Deathly Hallows*

As I wrote this book, many thoughts came to mind. I did not want to muddy the important part of the book with a lot of these things, but I felt they were worth mentioning. To that end, here is a collection of nuggets from the deep and shallow parts of my brain.

BOOBIES or DICK depending on taste: Do you

need to get someone's attention, so as not to start the next Armageddon over a simple task. I am the first to admit that I can zone out conversation if something is going on around me, easily focusing on the most important thing on my mind (while it is there). Just say Boobies in any tone and you will have that man's attention in literally a split second. As for women, they are always paying attention. That's why if you do something stupid, be upfront quickly to avoid the war of wars.

Some obvious ideas we don't think about or want to think about:

Skeletons in the closet can stay there unless they really need a little air. Just don't focus on them, they're dead and you don't live that way anymore, right?

Building a path: Is it going to be a smooth road or rocky one?

It's hard to fight naked!

Stand up for your Rights, and then sit down

because without a friend and a compromise, someone loses.

Don't wish for what you want! You just might get it and find out it tastes bad.

We can't live on bad memories and not look to the future for better times. Imagination is our most powerful tool.

There are times we listen as if it were elevator music.

No skin in the game? Kids, Debt, Medical, Money, Heartache. This isn't a game. Hate the game and the players for playing. Love your mate and best friend for staying.

What do you want, Bragging Rights?

No one can make you happy, they can only make it better.

One partner needs to learn to read, and the other should not write with a pen. Life is a pencil that we must keep sharp and take care of, so we don't have to keep sharpening it to find a new point to write with.

This is a journey I had to venture back into. A search of what we wrote about in our head that we made into reality. We are given a choice in life to explore what sets us apart and makes our internal A.I. either create with a pencil or write with a pen. Re-living our past that we were removed from has at least given us a picture of what our dream reality could end up being, if we weren't so busy writing the pages in Pen.

Is your life going to be a sitcom or a reality show?

Stay single they say, divorce is looked upon as a failure. So, if a widower was crashing into a divorce and they magically become a widower, the halo is awarded! Why does society put on us as humans, our **(kn)own** failures absolute?

Compare this list to the results that you checked off in Chapter 3. The Top 7 Reasons to Get Married:

1. Money
2. Love
3. Sex
4. Job
5. Happiness
6. Lifestyle
7. Car

The Top 7 Reasons to Get Divorced:

1. Lack of Money
2. No Love
3. No Sex or very little
4. No Job
5. No More Happiness- If you don't laugh and enjoy life, you will be Single
6. House to Homeless
7. Car Repossessed

Do you personally have a list you could conjure up

for either side of the argument of which there is only one winner? Why do we stop with all the charades once we get a partner? I get the car door opening, and I personally dropped that ball a long time ago, but the back rubs make up for that most of the time. I don't expect anyone to not have an argument, a fight, or a disagreement, but if you want this to work, then there has to be compromise (there's that word again). Or you can just live your favorite sitcom or cartoon and hope you get to watch the reruns when you get older.

The three vows of the evolved lover:

1. I will do my best to further the evolution of both myself and my partner towards higher consciousness, spiritual freedom, and increased soul growth.

2. I will always express unconditional love, for love's sake.

3. I will try to remember always to give you the freedom to be you, because out of love and respect, you give me the freedom to be me.

For many, marriage is a spiritual journey. Catholics

elevate it to the level of a sacred sacrament. The practice of love, compassion, understanding, and forgiveness goes a long way towards making any relationship stable and lasting.

The journey of love is an amazing one. It begins with self-love, not vanity or narcissism, but true respect for what thrives within you. The greatest warrior is one who conquers themselves. Self-love involves forgiveness of your past deeds, embracing who you are, and moving beyond any trauma that may have settled deep in your psyche. The past is gone. Accept that. To dwell in the past is to rob the present. If you are not happy living with yourself, you'll never be happy living with another person.

The next step on the journey is to love another, hence families. The demands of a family put us to the test, creating challenging situations that are best handled with love. Here we learn that we are love, loving, and beloved. If you had an unhappy childhood, let go of it now. It is in the past. You are free now. As science has taught us, we have as much to learn from failure as from success.

My friend Tony was a step child. His mother remarried three times before he graduated elementary school. When he grew up and married, he inherited step children from a previous marriage. When more children arrived, he made a rule that the word step-brother and step-sister would never be used. It was one of the ways he cemented the new family together, rising above the trauma of his early childhood to create his own vision of what a blended family would be like.

Beyond marriage and a partnership, the journey of love continues. We learn to love the people we see every day in our community. The friendly check-out person at the grocery store, the mailman, people at church, the next door neighbors. Love grows until we embrace patriotism and the love of our country. Ultimately we reach what is called agape, divine love, Christ Consciousness. It goes by many names, but at one point we realize we are all related, joined like brothers and sisters by the love of a benevolent God or at least a common acceptance of humaity. You will know you have reached this point when someone cuts you off in traffic and instead of getting angry you feel sorry for them. To be in such a hurry, such an angry state, unhappy for whatever reason, is sad. Forgive them, for they know not what they do.

All this from marriage? With the right person, anything is possible.

The Broadway Show that I sometimes imagine as my life is what I call the "Last Show of my Life". I am blessed to have finally found the Ying to my Yang. We have blended kids from 8 to 32 and it never gets boring. I have in-laws we caretake 12+ years. I might not have agreed with my future if I knew all the struggles we have endured together. How will your play be written? We are all actors, choose what character we will play, where the stage is going to be and what special guests are starring with you today. I can tell you that when we get together with our very collective group of other humans, it is like nothing you can see without a special ticket. Our slogan is "You can't pay for this kind of entertainment"

On our porch or Lanai as we say in the Islands. "If

you're not here, we will talk about you!"

I read quite a few Dr. Suess books in my day. Oh, the Places You Will Go..... If you were to look at the true meaning of his books, it is in life you will be tempted and you could have a bad reputation if you do the wrong thing. My answers and opinions are from my experiences both personal and within my circle that I created. No one person other than Jesus was perfect that I use in my circle of life. What will be your answers and opinions to someone that might use you as an example?

THE PROGRESSION OF TELEVISION

Note: No one but aging seniors really remembers these shows, but...

I loved Sitcoms such as *I Love Lucy*, *The Dick Van Dyke Show*, *The Honeymooners* and many more from the 60's. They had good and bad role models for us to learn from. They slept in separate beds, ate breakfast and dinner together, and what the heck, even had a full conversation.

Then it went south with The Golden Girls (we love and miss Betty White), with a bunch of women, some rich, and the others with just enough to get by. We know the characters well: the slut, the professional, the old funny lady, the high society lady, the blonde space case, and all the boyfriends and ex-husbands that moved in and out of their lives.

And now we have the lucky *Bachelorette*, *Sex in the City*, *Real Housewives*, *Wife Swap*, and even the all night adult hospital dramas.

So, if this last generation isn't messed up enough, even the cartoons have evolved in the same pattern. *Heckle and Jeckle*, *The Flintstones*, *The Jetsons*, *GI Joe* (one of the first cartoons specifically designed to sell action figures), *The Simpsons*, *Family Guy*, *Bob's Burgers*, and now the illustrious channels that feature toons like *Robot Chicken* and *Archer*. You get the point. We may laugh at these comical and dysfunctional characters, but what are we getting from them? What we bring into our brain (yes, the one we only use about ten percent of) finds a place to land and grow. If you don't think you have been personally hypnotized in your life, you are going to struggle without something solid to see, hear, or touch.

In my opinion the saddest progression is the journey of men and their television role models. We have gone from *Father Knows Best*, *My Three Sons*, and Ward on *Leave It To Beaver*, through Archie Bunker and Dennis Reynolds. Let's excuse Dick Solomon since he's only a visitor to the *Third Rock from the Sun*, but he's still not the role model I'm looking for. How about *Married With Children*? Doesn't that present a happy picture of life after being single? And *Everyone Loves Raymond*, but would you want to be married to him?

Eight Simple Rules with John Ritter was a blessing, even though he was less than the man of the house, he still provided a good role model. I liked John Goodman on the *Rosanne* show. For a short time I hung out with a group who liked to say, "We are the men we've been waiting for." That says it all for me. Goes right along with "Be the change in the world you want to see."

Chapter 7
Relationship and Marital Humor

I didn't come up with much humor here. There are a lot of critical and nasty jokes out there, but that's not what I'm about. Marriage may not be something to joke about, but I wanted to end this book with a laugh. Humor is the way we survive trauma and endure relationships. Jokes are usually about other people, but when we look and laugh at ourselves, we make this journey a little lighter for everyone. Laughter is the prelude to joy. May you always find joy in your life.

A young bride was preparing for her honeymoon. Her mother was helping her pack. "Don't forget to pack my pink nightgown," she said. "I want to wear it on my wedding night."

"Good choice," said Mom as she continued packing.

Having come from very traditional families, on the wedding night she and her husband were a little shy about getting dressed in front of each other. They had never seen each other naked. "I have an idea," said the husband. "I'll get dressed in the other room and you get dressed here."

"Okay," said the nervous bride.

"And no peeking!" warned the husband.

They went about their tasks. The wife opened her suitcase only to find that her mother had stuffed the nightgown in it. She pulled it out and held it up. "Ahhhh!" she screamed. "It's all pink and wrinkly."

From the other room came the reply. "You peeked! You peeked!"

***

Heard on the Johnny Carson Tonight Show one night as he was interviewing famous golf pro

Arnold Palmer's wife: “Do you do anything to give him luck before a game?”

“Oh, yes,” she answered. “I kiss his balls.”

To which Johnny replied. “I bet that makes his putter stand on end.”

I wonder how Johnny came up with some of his questions. On another occasion he asked a woman, “What would you do if your husband was suddenly turned into a giant bird?”

“I'd put newspapers down on the floor,” she said.

***

This couple decided to not go to bed angry with each other. At the next marriage counseling session they told the therapist.

“That's great,” he said. “How’s that working out for you?”

“We haven’t slept in three days.”

Okay, enough joking around. Here are some more to enjoy at a website that I liked:

https://www.boredpanda.com/married-life-jokes/

I believe that life is more then they told us it would be.

I will live with the rules of our house that keep us grounded to each other out of respect and compromise.

No Lying

No Stealing

No Secrets

Will any of these rules affect my friendship?

I want to hear your stories of life to share.

Thank you for reading.

www.sevendaymarriage.com

PART II

WORKSHEETS TO ACCOMPANY THE "MARRIAGE"

DAY 1 WORKSHEET

Don't you just love it when you get to a town or city and go into a random coffee house and the service was amazing, almost fairy tale amazing. That makes the rest of my day so awesome.

This is the beginning of the journal of your Seven Day Marriage. You are writing your story. These will be memories, good or bad, that will last beyond a mere seven days. You can refer to these pages when you need to look back and look at yourself and what you did with your best friend.

To help you get started, answer these simple questions:

What did you do today?

What did you see?

What did you do for lunch? What was the conversation like?

Name at least one compliment you got and one you gave. Where were you when it happened?

Did you kiss in public?

Did you buy anything today?

Was there anything you wish you didn't see?

Did you do anything you were ashamed of?

Name something funny that happened today.

Get the idea? Try making up your own questions to ask each other. Write them down on the next page along with your answers.

Enjoy the day getting to know each other especially if you just met this person and want to spend the rest of your life with them. It Happens every day!!!

I have faithfully followed the rules of the Seven Day Marriage Today _________ (initial)

I broke the following rule(s): ______ (initial)

DAY 2 WORKSHEET

How did the day go? Is there anything you need to talk about over dinner or some evening cocktails? What did you do today that you enjoyed? What was the best part of the day? Don't just say being with you is all I need. If you get to this point on the first day then, you might want to rethink if you want a baby and you're the parent.

Was there anything you felt uncomfortable talking about today? Did you avoid the subject?

That said, write down today's experience. What did you do, see, eat, wish you didn't see? Evaluate your own feelings and behaviors. Was there anything that made you uncomfortable? Happy? Appreciated?

I have faithfully followed the rules of the Seven Day Marriage Today _________ (initial)

I broke the following rule(s): ______ (initial)

DAY 3 WORKSHEET

"Good morning my Love" again and again every day whether together or not.

This is awesome and we are excited to do what is next on the journey. Today we are going to work on our sight sense as this can be the most important one. If you haven't watched the movie Shallow Hal, then you just might want to watch it if this doesn't make sense.

Unless you are a doctor that forgot to take a vacation or you are the President, you didn't make this important enough to sign a lifetime commitment. The first thing you are going to do after professing your love for each other, you are going to leave your cell phone, beepers, and any device other than a camera to record your trip today. Leave it at home, I mean anywhere but in reach. This is the no distractions type of a journey to explore the person you are going to live with for the rest of your life! You are now going to take at least 10 minutes 3 times today and just look into the other persons eyes. You can hold hands, but you need to be just sitting on a beach, mountain, by the lake, even in a crowd of people. You will be completely still like a mime. I love when people stare at us in public because then I know I can always sell tickets to my Broadway play.

What did you do, see, eat, wish you didn't see?

I have faithfully followed the rules of the Seven Day Marriage Today _________ (initial)

I broke the following rule(s): _______ (initial)

DAY 4 WORKSHEET

On this day, I want you to write down on this worksheet the things you love about them; for instance, the post-it note on your car wheel, the breakfast in bed, the foot rub, and so. But on the other side, we want to discover the things we can't deal with or need to compromise on. You need to be individuals that work together. If you want to be a slave, then I guess that makes you happier. Not me!

GO! List 5 things you like about this person:

1

2

3

4

5

Now list 5 things you don't like or can't compromise on

1

2

3

4

5

Think of a way you can compromise on just 3 of these things.

1

2

3

What would you change about this person if you could?

What would you change about yourself if you could?

Now you are going to write a sentence or paragraph on why you both are on this journey. If you can't communicate this today, what makes you think it is going to just magically work out for both of you? It might be stupid to one person and make the world of difference to the other.

I have faithfully followed the rules of the Seven Day Marriage Today ________ (initial)

I broke the following rule(s): ______ (initial)

DAY 5 WORKSHEET

“Good morning my Love” again and again everyday whether together or not. I shouldn’t even be putting this down, because you should be doing this like you were taking your last breath.

Today I feel like (check as many as you like):

□ I can be in love forever

□ This is my soul mate

□ I feel like running and hiding

□ We have compromised well in the past few days

□ Why did I agree to this?

□ I have learned something

□ There is no way I can make this work

□ I'm confused

□ At least I get a vacation out of it

- ☐ I don't like the way they ______________________
- ☐ We don't communicate
- ☐ I find them an interesting person
- ☐ This can only go down hill from here
- ☐ I'm exhausted
- ☐ I'm having trouble revealing my percieved faults
- ☐
- ☐
- ☐
- ☐
- ☐

Write a journal entry describing your day:

I have faithfully followed the rules of the Seven Day Marriage Today ________ (initial)

I broke the following rule(s): ______ (initial)

DAY 6 WORKSHEET

"Good morning my Love" again and again everyday whether together or not. Are we getting the point yet, that this is a contract for life? It's not a car loan on something that, if not well maintained, is just going to break down and then all you want to do or think about is the new model that is available.

Today's lesson is what would you like to do for our next 1-year goal and 5-year goal.

Where do you see yourself (and your partner) in a year?

Where do you see yourself (and your partner) in five years?

I have faithfully followed the rules of the Seven Day Marriage Today _________ (initial)

I broke the following rule(s): ______ (initial)

DAY 7 WORKSHEET

“Good morning my Love”, if you haven’t yet.

We should be at the peak of happiness or glad to get home and kiss the dog, cat, whatever. I hope you had the most wonderful time like I did with my wife to this day and until I die. Thank God I tried this idea of mine and it worked. I have shared this idea with at least 20 close friends and acquaintances that have been together for 20 to 60 years. Over time, they all had similar ideas, keeping friendship as number one. Because of the foundation, we join into this sacred union as one. We want to recognize that it takes two people to make this work.

Do you have what it takes?

Have you learned anything as a result of your Seven Day Marriage?

Your lesson today is to decide if you are going to sign a real contract and commit to each other like we were built to do: with our mind, body, and spirit.

Or will you go separate ways?

No matter what you choose, you will be happy with your decision. You will have learned something you didn't know before, either about yourself or your partner.

I have faithfully followed the rules of the Seven Day Marriage Today _________ (initial)

I broke the following rule(s): ______ (initial)

DAY 8 AND BEYOND

Is the outcome what you wanted or expected? Write down your thoughts.

If you were successful and are now planning a life together, stop reading! Put the book down and go have happily ever after. Thanks for reading!

Now, if that didn't happen and you are now back to where you started, consider these things:

You are not back where you started. You learned something. You avoided a costly mistake. You did your best.

Now, review your journal from this week. Think about your answers. Were you true to yourself? (yes, answer this question now)

Are you ready to try again? Do you have any worthy candidates for another Seven Day Marriage?

Do you have a support team, a friend, relative, or someone to discuss this with?

What are you going to do to move forward?

It's hard not to, but try not to blame yourself if things didn't work out. There are a lot of reasons that people don't want to get married, almost as many as they do. Maybe they didn't share something from their past. Maybe they weren't "marriage material". Maybe there are a thousand reasons to call it off. Here is a partial list:

	I've had a bad marriage before and don't want a repeat of that experience
	I don't have enough patience to compromise
	Marriage is a trap
	I'm a confirmed bachelor(ette)
	I will lose my Government benefits if I get married
	Why buy the cow when you get the milk for free?
	It's too expensive. I can't afford the ring
	I don't trust them (or myself)
	I'm a non-committal kind of person
	I don't want to be a burden to anyone
	They can't cook
	I'm marrying their debt
	I know it won't last
	Do I still get to keep the ring?
	Everything's fine. Why spoil it by getting married?
	I'm afraid
	I have baggage and I can't unload it
	They have baggage and I can't deal with it
	Let's just forget this ever happened

	Too many red flags
	We're fire and ice, oil and vinegar, just not compatible
	I'm still legally married to someone else
	Let's just wait until (some future promise occurs)
	I like a long engagement
	I'm (or you're) poly-amorous and you're (I'm) not
	I don't dance and I don't want to embarrass you at a wedding
	You want me to what?
	I can't think of any reason why we should get married (and other excuses)
	I'm convinced that nobody could ever love me
	We will get married when I get out of prison
	Your pet/kids hate me. It's either them or me.
	You are not my soul mate
	You had an affair even though we were engaged
	I learned something about you I can't live with
	I learned something about myself and I don't want marriage

If that's not enough to get you moving, go back to basics. Just consider that it wasn't you. Try not to assign blame. Things just happened that way. Don't play the victim. You already know where that gets you.

If you feel depressed, you have to get up and move. Despair and the many forms it takes just want to make you sit down and do nothing. Maybe wallow in misery. If you get up and take a walk it will go away. The act of moving your body introduces chemicals that drive that feeling away.

When I was a teenager whining to my mother about a bad romance, she had these words to say. “When you were a baby, I watched you try to learn to walk. You would take a few steps and fall down. Sometimes you would cry for a minute, but always you would get up and walk again.”

The thought of never learning to walk and me still crawling around like an infant made me laugh.

Just as it is our destiny to walk upright, it is our destiny to love again. After all, we are human. We cannot deny our capacity to love and be loved.

I challange you to try again. Accept that you are human and move on. Today is still the first day of the rest of your life. We don't always achieve our goals the first time we try.

I have a friend who likes to say, “Love is like a mathematical equation. It takes time to figure it out."

Give yourself some time. In the meantime, go do something you like to do. It's still your adventure. Happy people tend to attract other happy people. I bet you won't be alone for long.

Thank you for reading.

www.ingramcontent.com/pod-product-compliance
Lightning Source LLC
LaVergne TN
LVHW010624100826
845148LV00014B/3097
* 9 7 8 1 5 8 8 8 4 0 2 9 5 *